POEMS OF LOVE AND LOSS

Edward Jones

for Beryl

Edward Jones

This collection copyright Edward Jones 2012
ISBN 978-1-4717-2674-3
First published 2012

Set in 11/14 Garamond
Typesetting and design by Liz French, liz@lizfrench.co.uk

Published by Edward Jones

Contents

Love and Loss

Prelude	11
Odysseus 1	12
Odysseus 2	13
Penelope 1	14
Penelope 2	15
Student Union, Durham, 1949	16
Palace Green, Durham, 1949	17
Shincliffe Hall, Durham, 1949	18
Authorpe 1952	20
Return to the Old Rectory, Authorpe (1998-1952)	22
Watford, 1955	25
Monument: Thetford Chase, 1960	26
You 1968	27
You	28
Departure 1968	30
Interlude 1	31
Freesias	32
Icarus	33
I think of you	34
You were not...	36
Interlude 2	37
Summer gone	38
Light out of dark	39
Do not speak	40

Solitaries	41
Higher degree	42
On the beach	43
In the shallows	44
On Waxham beach	46
Climate change	48
Your silence	49
Changing places	50
Gathering	51

Musical Offerings

Songs without words	54
Our song	55
Music and Silence	56
Music of the heart	57
A musical offering	58
Impromptu	60
Slow movement: *andante con moto*	61
Key signature	62
Last song: No 3 Richard Strauss	63
Last Song: No 4 Richard Strauss	64
Partita	66

In France

To my children from Provence	68
Le Murillon	69
Toulon waterfront	70
Ales	72
Under the vine	73

Poems of Love and loss

With Reference to God

Duino	76
Quaker meeting 1	77
Quaker meeting 2	78
Quaker meeting 3	79
I never understood	80
Those who love	81
What You are	82
But if it's true	83
Getting to know You	84
Not knowing	85
Even if one	86

Other poems

Words to Rilke	88
Letters	89
Autumn	90
Dawn 1962	91
Russian lessons 1958	92
Marking time	94

Index of titles   95

Love and Loss

Edward Jones

Love and Loss

Prelude

There was a song waiting to be sung.
No one had heard it, and its theme
Existed only in the provinces of dream.
No manuscript recorded it; no voice
Beguiled it in the subtle web of rhyme.
And yet, its not existing was so strong
That forms of possibility required
We two should sing it into time.

This was no simple human choice.
All was insisted upon. Pure sense
Demanded to become; and so desired
Was that insistence that your voice
Took shape, took wing; grew so intense
That possibility became experience.

Odysseus 1

Why should he not, old voyager,
Sponsored by gods and goddesses, expect
That, in the Olympian scheme of things,
It was he, bold thrusting warrior,
Who bore the weight of all that destiny?

So many dawns, so many miles,
So many epic-stepping isles!
Why should he not assume,
Across the oceans' drift and spume,
That it was he who held the key?
Though all the while it was, and had been, she;
That Other, his much-neglected, old,
That stay-at-home, his mild Penelope,
Becoming, as he neared her, Youth; becoming Gold;
Becoming Eternity.

Odysseus 2

So, then did he, the master voyager,
Experience afresh, and every single time,
The coarse-grained deck boards at his feet,
The twitch of rigging and the caustic smell of sea,
When, yet again, and with a diminished crew,
He slipped the latest reef
And headed home for Ithaca?

Or, as once more they cleared
Another harbour mouth, and jeered
Defeated Cyclops raging from the hill,
Was there, as part of his experience,
Some tug of doubt, some taint of fear
Of that long-drawn-out haul of peace approaching;
Domestic expectation and the rule of law?
And central to all this, with no escaping,
The innocent, unchanging purity
Of Penelope awaiting?

Penelope 1

When, faithful and dying, his old dog, Argus, raised
His head, and limped into the mid-day glare,
She knew that it was happening.

Earlier, she'd felt her handmaids' sideways stare,
And in her glass found Time's accumulated evidence erased.
She trembled for its fading.

Trembled, too, for him who soon would bear
The weight of her relentless purity invading:
Gathered by years and by loneliness refined.

After the upheaval of the banquet hall,
Footsteps would sound, her latch would lift and fall.
His eyes, by sun and ocean blind,
Might almost fail to sight her shadowed waiting;
Her loom at rest, her hands at last reposing.

She trembled for him and for the diminishment
She would impose, and could not help imposing.

She turns her head. As though from infinitely far,
He feels the flaming comet of his lust abating,
Engulfed by the gravity of her dark star.
His multitudinous miles, erotic loves, exotic shores,
All magical enchantments for ever closing.

Lost in the simple opening of her door.

Penelope 2

She'd been expecting him since waking,
Hands folded on her timeless waiting.
Round her, discarded threads accumulating;
Blood crimsons tamed at every night's unbraiding.

She'd woven him across the oceans' loom:
The salt-sharp greens, the overarching blues.
Sun-flash on steel, scarlet of sirens' calling;
Cerulean Circe's poisonous masquerading.

He was coming, he was near,
Fashioned to his ultimate landfall
By yesterday's last nightfall weaving.
Early dawning's faded strands
Abandoned flotsam on her dark room floor.

Grey morning, tied and threaded, waiting.
Soon she would work his dispossession's landing
On grey unsmiling homeland. The crowded hall.
Last fiery threads of vengeance falling.
The corridor.

And then the opening of her door.

Student Union, Durham, 1949

Your uncle's summons from on high
Came from a clear and unsuspecting sky.
From that time on, stranger to doubt and fear,
He did God's work for more than fifty years.
Miracle? Family joke? Both, maybe.
I, no less abruptly called, honour the mystery.

Revelation is a tricky word, mine an unlikely case,
Yet how else name it, when a face,
Glimpsed once, and briefly, immediately proposes
Possibilities which life disposes
Right then, and just exactly where
Nothing existed but emptiness, despair?

Mid-term, mid-winter, life between
Approximate past and future every bit as mean
And meagre as the rations we still drew;
Tokens of war we still submitted to.
Only you youngsters, bright and new,
Signalled up hope. I should have noticed you
Earlier, no more than half concealed,
(A profile or a rearward view).

But only when two youthful heads withdrew
Just for a moment were you revealed.
Your open forehead, rusting Autumn hair,
Your wide-set eyes, alive to all things there
Apart from me, distinct as any summoning voice,
Offering no soft option and as little choice.
Certainly no chance to bargain or dispute;
This one was final. Absolute.

Palace Green, Durham, 1949

We made post-war austerity a fashion.
We wore ex-Service greatcoats, and battledress
With faded patches: memorials to rank and function
We temporarily assumed.
We were free but could not quite possess
Our freedom.

The place we occupied was no-man's land.

Huddled in doorways from the sniping hail,
We watched as you sure-footed through the mines
Of cobbled ice (later to ambush you
And leave its marks for life).
We were not sure enough
To know if we should sneer or applaud.

You wore poverty as if it was a promise:
Your overcoat made up from blackout stuff;
Your almost schoolgirl uniform, such threadbare
Camouflage! How could it diminish or disguise
Your forward-facing march to everywhere?

Shincliffe Hall, Durham, 1949

'Bombers' Moon' we would have called it,
Five years earlier, quick to appropriate
Nature to our immediate concerns.
We knew about the nakedness of power;
And we were all naked under that scouring light,
Hunter and hunted.

Walking you home, I felt its tidal pull.
If I had dropped my guard, it would have sucked me
Up through the night sky's circular incision,
Along with all the colour, light and life
The roads and fields and hedges had surrendered.

You could not know, and I would not acknowledge,
The terror of that draw, that majestically indifferent
Attraction. I held your arm,
Dreading my journey home.

'Lovers' Moon' you would have preferred,
And could have quoted sources.
You saw silver, you saw frosted fantasies;
The already beautiful splendidly enhanced.
That was your way. To everything
You brought your magical enchantment.

You were my 'Lovers' Moon'.
I was flooded by your benign illumination.

Love and Loss

Except that I was all too anxiously aware,
Decades away from Rilke, that beauty
Operated on the edge of terror;
And my interior landscape was quite bare
Of anything your searching light could work upon.
Hollow, I was doubly exposed, doubly terrorised.

Twin moons, you both were full that night,
And I, solitary orbiter, experienced
Your full unmoderated beams right through me.

Authorpe, 1952

Noises map the countryside at night.
Particular barking, screaming, cries
Pinpoint familiar terrain for the seasoned ear.

No trouble, then, for you! Your Wiltshire years,
The Causeway's Roman miles,
The loneliness, the dark,
The rats, the middens, the incestuous lives.
You were well equipped for our rural trials.

'Something's trapped', you said, that night,
Our first. It seemed a reasonable view,
Given the state of that decaying wall,
The cretin offspring, the pig-man's alien tongue.
I had no cause to disagree with you.
The trap I'd stepped in seemed already sprung.

In a hard bed, in a cold room, we clung,
The house collapsing, mice quartering the floor,
And held each other, while the unknown plunged
And threshed. 'Not trapped,' I said. 'Emerging!'

Why not? Out of that ancient shaft, that surging,
Anything could have surfaced, could have reared,
Deposited itself in our backyard.
Though not grotesque enough to cap my urban fears.

Love and Loss

And yet, next morning, smiling and benign,
Lincolnshire dismissed our worries; yours and mine.

Except that, in the yard, at our backdoor,
In place of the well and its crude brick wall,
And the rusting pump in its wooden suit,
Handle curved like a monkey's tail,
There was a hole. Almost neat. Undramatically small.
It looked so innocent! Not threatening at all.
But till they filled it in, I kept a wary eye,
Reflecting how precarious we were,
How temporary, how new.
Anonymous visitors just passing through.

Return to the Old Rectory, Authorpe (1998-1952)

Never suppose that I was unaware,
Those long hard years, that it was you
Who held our stumbling infant world together.
Think, rather, that I did not dare
Admit conditions I had pledged you to:
Wrecked house, its best years gone,
Heavy loneliness, a barely thriving child,
Blank isolation, and the fear that must have stalked
Your future, recently bestowed on one
Whose hold on life itself was weak, unsure,
As grip of hand on water.

Only now, a lifetime's trek away,
And recollecting, as I must, that given day
When we, on impulse (could it have been otherwise?),
Went back, imposed our will on time;
Bore witness to this present through older eyes;
And found the railway swept away,
The church impossibly removed, the graveyard stones
Falling, fallen into deep decay.
Only now can I, in part and fleetingly, contrive
To grasp some shadow of what it all might mean;
What Rilke had proposed for bees, those workers who,
Trawling the Visible, the current scene,
Accumulate their harvest in the golden hive
Of the Invisible. Oh, You! Oh You!
You worker bee whom I would call my Queen!

For it was still there, just recognizably,
That tired old house, wearing its new disguise;
In no way proud, but not apologetically,
Though two or three times grown beyond its former size.

Still there! The meeting line of bricks,
The roof extended. These almost deceived the sight,
And might have but for one small window right
Where I had stood, naked and half-aware,
Barefoot on uncovered boards
And rocked a restless child to sleep.

We climbed the well-remembered stairs
And at the second bend, just where
A still-protruding extra step was placed
To guide unwary feet into that space
We'd used to store the water tank and apples,
A wide expanse of cupboards stopped us short
To cry aloud together,
'Look, still there!'

Feeling the heart of that old house,
I came to see what you'd been doing
Through those interminable days
Of long bare Wolds approaching winter skies;
Or golden swathes of summer grain,
And summer heat and all-enfolding light.

You'd harvested that world, that visible domain:
Ruth upright amid alien corn,
Mary pondering all things in her heart;

Your female soul internalising all
This coarse and transitory stuff that Rilke sang
As plunging into profound Being.
Only, it seemed, with you, not plunging,
But settling. Becoming. Being!

Love and Loss

Watford, 1955

Saturdays, our neighbours manicured their lawns,
In due order, mower, roller, shears.
Sundays, they shampooed their cars:
A sober Sabbath ceremony.
So why did it bother me,
This easy target for my sneers?

From the far country of almost fifty years,
I ask myself: how did we appear?
Neglected garden, posters boasting CND;
Press photos of our two boys and me,
Militant behind a banner.
And Sundays, high on morality,
I trundled Roy, grossly spastic seventeen,
Down from Leavesden Hospital
In an iron cart. Home for tea.

Kindly folk they must have been,
Still grappling post-war anxieties.
Too young to have played a part
In the first war. Too old for the second.
For them no visionary future beckoned.
So why not scrub decks and polish brass,
Secure the hawsers of a confined destiny?
We were the strangers. We would pass.

Monument: Thetford Chase, 1960

They had not expected to be there,
Name, rank and number,
Chipped on a grey stone base.
Incongruous in that unassuming place;
Monument to stupendous folly.
They'd never looked to play a part
In any epic enterprise;
Not even be remembered, much less memorialised.

I had not expected to be there,
On A11, leaning on that stone,
While larks erupted and insects droned,
And all around the forest lay in waiting.

Washed into a land so docile, so benign,
That register of open farms and skies,
I took no comfort from the sign
That welcomed us to Norfolk.

I had always taken it as read,
And followed blindly as of right,
A course had been marked out for me,
Plotted across parks and squares and roads and railway lines,
On that over-used and dog-eared chart,
Scribbled and marginally amplified;
The city dweller's pride,
Searched and scoured and confidently read:
My battered text; my London A to Z.

You 1968

You with your fond capacious womb
Encompass all. You give to me
Five lives whose youthful beauties bloom
Like roses; there for all to see:
Monuments to your capacity.

You with your warm attentive grace
Encourage all. As flowers to the sun,
To you, the longed-for, welcome place,
Bereft or starving creatures run;
And find what they need doing, done.

You with your full unchecked assent
Accomplish all. Why, then, surprise,
That, loving as you do to this extent,
Of lovers and of love's new enterprise
You can accommodate infinities?
I, with my fond enraptured heart
Admit your full capacity;
Expect of your wide love no single part
Exclusively assigned by you to me,
Except what grows by your most going free.

You

You are not God, and loving you,
Though probing furthest frontiers of this world,
Seems not of heaven.

Your signals home
Compel my system's full capacity
To codify the mysteries you fly among:
The many-headed monsters and the sirens' song.
But all within my humankind technology.

I check equipment. Daily rounds
Confirm the functions of my circuit board.
This is my part, preparing ground
To which shall come your wholly human word.

Nights, though, across my screen,
Insistent signals of a further range
Disturb. I find receivers changed
By messages they're programmed to record.

Loving, it seems, means being changed.
Not changing: being changed.

With reference to God, this changing stuff
Is all as humans we can bring to bear:
Maintain alertness, clear the air;
Switch gear to ease incoming tones.

Love and Loss

Technicians, we ensure the way
Is unimpaired; and for the rest,
We influence neither message nor its source.
Both these belong at levels of command
Beyond our rank or reach.

Let's labour, then, to keep the networks clear;
Accessible to that influence which,
Intelligible to neither mind nor ear,
Makes of each separate self a universe;
Of eternity, the living now and here.

Departure 1968

Soon as your plane has gone,
My scattered remnants of identity
Hang like kerosene in the London sky.

Crossing the crowded lounge, I know
It would be like this if you had died.
I clutch a counter hawking plastic ties,
And tell my small obituaries.

Not for you.
Your completeness death can merely ratify.

Driving home, I think of you;
Always think of you as a child
Knee-deep in the Wiltshire wind.

In my loneliness I long to comfort that solitary child
I never knew,
Creating a self out of the Roman miles.

Perhaps as a child I could have loved you
In the way I want to love:
Able to feel an equal one.

I have walked knee-deep through your winds
A lifetime, looking for what a war-time child once found.

Now I reach home, and all around,
The Roman legions of your love
Engulf me.

Interlude 1

Before I met you,
It was not so much a case of being lost,
As not being there at all;

Except for those small scraps
Of what might constitute my being
You salvaged and set upon a path
Where they might flourish and not fall.

What that path was, and where it might be leading,
I did not know.
But I was conscious, and beyond all measure
Grateful, that possibilities arose
Which I might grapple.

After that, there was always present,
As a sub-text, a scarcely-noticed other;
Some fleeting, never-to-be-captured,
Almost-scent, almost-taste;
An atmosphere, an affirmation
That things were well and could get better.

To what purpose I was so engaged
Could, remarkably, be set aside.
I was content to let things ride.
Once I had you,
How could things not be good and true?

Freesias

When did you throw those freesias away,
Bought on a market stall, dead the second day?
I could have sworn I smelled them in the room.

Light thickens as the day ends.
Over the trees, shadows soak the remaining sun.
Walls, fabrics, books along the shelves
Keep something of the day's occasional beams.

All contributes; nothing is lost.
If you die first, I shall come in here
And start to ask you about flowers.
It won't be you. I won't surprise you
Hanging around, fearful for my lonely state.
I've finally released you from all that.
Nor memory, either, the simple longing of a life
You mostly formed.
I shan't be keeping you from that daunting place
Your passage is already booked to.

Purpose is what you'll leave; accumulated sense
Of spirit moving towards other Being;
Hard-won, a lifetime's essence, one drop of which
Will surely our multitudinous seas incarnadine.

In minds of those you love,
As flowers and sun and sprays of music
Played once and never heard again,
You've changed the complexion of this turning world.

Icarus

'Never look directly at the sun',
They said. 'You'll lose your sight.
And as for counting stars at night,
Be sure to eye them seemingly askance;
Approach them surreptitiously, as one
Might come upon them, as it were, by chance'.

Yes, but astronomic revelation beckoned.
Who cared if pride should prophesy a fall?
I drew my shallow courage in and staked it all;
I fixed my puny wings and leapt.
Never doubting, up I went; and kept
Straight for the sun. If not for the heart of it, I reckoned,
Why leap at all?

Nobody was watching, they were getting on with things:
Exchanging books, drinking, most likely arguing.
If someone had told them what I aimed to do,
They'd have fallen down laughing, as I'd expect them to.
How could they know that I was focused straight on you?

Nothing is as blind as love
Felt by the weak for the supremely strong.
Dazzled I was by your refining fire.
But boosted by this thought, I blundered up above:
"Does not the ultimately pure require
Earth elements coarse-grained, mongrel, stained,
If that essential purity's to remain
True centre, the circling stars among?"

As for the Pleiades, their exact count
Remains, for me at least, in doubt.
But there they are, and countless lesser stars,
Not to mention Saturn, Jupiter and Mars,
Offering themselves to be sung about.

Blinded by love, I'll orbit you. Your gravity
Will draw me close, closer, to where I'm meant to be.

I think of you

I have been thinking of you all day.
I think about you every day, of course.
Sometimes I think you are my thought,
So closely you inhabit me.
Indeed, I think I could be satisfied....
Your death not yet a year away....
If we could stay like this forever:
The two of us together,
Curiously united, inextricably simplified.

But the February sun has shone all day;
The sky has stayed a clear unaltered blue
For one whole week, while in the park,
Celandines and crocuses, springing through,
Face sunwards, anticipating Spring.
And I, survivor of the winter's dark,
Observe new growth and change in everything.

It would be easy to suppose that this rebirth,
This seasonal triumph over death,
is one of Nature's more kindly metaphors
For human lives; for mine and yours.

But buds are buds, and next time round,
They'll still be buds emerging into flowers.
Symbols of continuity, perhaps. Not ours!
For buds and tender shoots and ocean tides and stars
Comprise the wheel on which we're temporarily bound.
They are the wheel and cannot modify
Their pattern of obligatory rotation.

That is their limitation and their compensation.
While we, lacking such unarguable certainty,
Are quite otherwise intended,
Mysterious as we are, and open-ended;
Open to every possibility:
To dissolution or wondrous transformation;
Oblivion or eternity.

You were not...

You were not teaching me,
Though I was ready to be taught.
You were not leading me,
Though I was more than keen to follow.
You were enabling me to be.

You were not criticising me,
Though I was ready to be scorned.
Nor even praising me when I did well,
Though I was eager for your approbation.

Everything was given, right at the start.
All was *for*given, for your heart
Encompassed even my unfaithfulness. You knew
That faithfulness was something I was growing to.

Interlude 2

A kind of interlude within your journey.
A seeming pause in your soul's breathing,
I felt no shame that I should thus impede
The so-serene proceeding of your spirit.

Towards the end of your sweet staying,
I had become the proper host. I was made free
To bring you food and drink and shelter.
I knelt before you and I washed your feet;
Finding at last a perfect freedom
In service which confirmed equality.

I did my welcoming as you were making to depart.

Now you are gone and I have swept the floor
I knelt on; laundered and put to dry
The towels; hidden the French expensive soap
I would insist on buying.
The house is empty but retains
What I can only, at this moment, call your shadow,
If shadows can be full of light and grace.

It's how your absence steals upon me
As I sit at night: warm and confiding.
Your wordless legacy.

Summer gone

Summer gone and you gone.
What, of my long life with you,
Stays whole, unambiguously true?

Not memory, that fickle friend
Of light forgetfulness; register of the dead;
Uneasy witness to uneasy starts, unlikely ends.
Communications wilfully misread.
Fugitive, Proust called it; as are the years!
Vault of lost hopes, abandoned fears.

Each of us a Valley of the Kings
Randomly plundered: ancestral relics, rings
On fingers of always-fading ghosts.
Unsatisfactory evidence of departed things.
Too-distant echo of voices longed-for most.

Why, even Proust, fine-tuned to spot the mark
Of hidden hoards, plays only temporary host
For the buried dark to be a little less than dark.

And humankind, the poet says, can bear
Only a little reality; and there
He touches on a truth.
But oh, that little, that spare,
That almost unbelievably rare!
Those moments of the now-more-than-ever-you,
Whole and sure and absolutely true!

Light out of dark

You never stooped to pity me;
Would not confer that last dependency;
Though I might well have wished its consolation.

For you already knew
That my particular salvation
Would only come when you
Became dependent, full and clear, on me.

Your last and silent years
Were your most precious gift;
Allowed our customary roles to be reversed,
As though reliance was something you'd rehearsed
To show the world in your tranquillity,
That I had gained equality,
And we had proved, together, love's supremacy.

Do not speak

Do not speak,
And if you would reach me,
Hum.

Words act as fence posts in a field;
Anchorage in water;
Snagging detritus of particular lives.
They peg with thought-lines what we want to fly.

Do not speak,
And if you would reach me,
Sigh.

I chewed my way to you
Through woods of words.
Now there is open range
And unencumbered sky.

Do not speak,
And if you would reach me,
Cry.

Solitaries

Rilke was right to call us bees.
Bees gather, so must we.
But human energy
Is randy for dispersal:
    no sooner in than out,
    seen than interpreted,
    experienced than shared.
We are the great distributors:
Points of sale, depots, department stores.
The Marks and Spencers of inheritance.

Consider, then, the solitary ones;
Honour their loneliness,
The dignity of their accumulation.
Assembly points, poles of attraction,
The lives of solitaries assume a shape:
    levels of silence,
    weight of endured space,
    climate of stillness.

I often think that in some cosmic Mind
Original creation is performed
In every individual.
And solitary souls acquire:
    as moss on stone,
    petals on a lawn,
    sunlight and the press of wind,
Just as this turning world did once in solitude,
Their gravity, their weight, their special atmosphere.

Higher degree

Why did I talk of joy; the pure response
To academic grasp? My mind
Was far away on other things.
And yet it served; the neutral,
Non-attached, uncircumscribed experience
Was exact; existed whole, itself.
To think of definition was absurd.

Mornings, I wake, lie, hear you stir.
You gone, I potter, tackle dishes,
Wander town-wards, clear snow.
Turn pages of those hard-used days
Whose dust exhales a sense
Of absolute precision undefined.

Each moment's print comes clear
Through finger stains, through blots,
Through comment pencilled in some unknown hand.

On the beach

A place for me to wait and watch
To see if I might catch,
Far out, the thinnest line of blue,
Signalling distant sun preparing to break through;
And wonder if I might sense the slightest hint of joy,
When, hitherto,
Joy had its only residence in you.

In the shallows

On this bald coast where earth and ocean slide
Obscurely into shared identity,
I stand apart in shallow water,
Poised between rising dunes and falling deep.
I am conscious of the stance I keep
On shifting sand; holding the middle ground.

I think of Rilke and Cezanne,
Poet and painter who would not allow
Distinctive separation of the senses;
And Proust, whose artist, Estril, painted land
In terms of sea; sea in respect of land.

From where I stand, I see you in the dunes,
Almost disguised as shuffling grass and sand.
Sun-haze involves you with the wind and scent of salt,
And children's voices; and the wheeling dance
Of time held motionless, and space for ever caught.

There is apparent peace in shallow waters.
Children may play there; the old
Lift their worn skirts and for now re-live
Moments such as even harshest lives must hold.

But shallows afford no permanent retreat;
I feel the current changing, and the flow
Turning to ebb. And at my back I know
The pull, the dark oblivion of the deep.

While up ahead, light concentrates itself,
So dazzling that it seems to rise
Past now-abandoned pools and ridge of shells
And pebbled bank to climbing dunes;
And draws aloft its very heart; away
To where you are,
Now like some announcing star,
Eclipsing summer's brightening day.

On Waxham beach

I am drawn back to this raw beach,
Routinely scourged by thin North Easter's claw,
Which rakes the contours of this barren shore,
And spurs the ocean rollers' furthest reach
Of tide-line whitened bones and polished stones and shells,
Junked by these vast indifferent swells;
And sends the whitening grasses genuflecting to the West.

Here, wind is king; permits no distinction and no rest;
Only perpetual movement which disperses and enfolds,
Scatters and assembles, occasionally lulls and holds
This space, this time, and our too-wintering selves.

Far out, grey sky and ocean merge
To hang like faded linen, angling tears
Across the promontory's primal urge
To hump its nuclear burden's surge
To where the sea and sky and sand and billowed air
Are one encompassing, shifting blur.

There are no children's voices from the dunes.
No holiday laughter of summer afternoons.

Sand-blown, we lay; sun-drenched and love-dazed;
Observed the shifting silhouettes of ships upraised
Mid-air among the indefinite August haze;
Land stealthily hinting at itself. Shadowly appraised,
Sizewell miraged in heat extruded from this ancient land;
Groynes groping seaward from dissolving sand.

Love and Loss

Here we encounter life's enlightenment:
No rounded certainties; only the human what-might-be;
Our fragile selves cast up, discarded by life's tidal flow
On this one moment's shore. Mingled and whirled about,
No outlines sharp, not of the self nor of the stuff
Our everyday is made of. No discrete identity.
This is the place for Turner and his 'Fighting Temeraire';
All substance dissolving in the uncertain air.

I walked your beach a life entire.
I opened my arms, my heart, to your wind's desire,
Blowing me Southerly, Southerly.

I melted in your sun's refining fire,
Growing me Otherly, Otherly.

I dream of cosmic wind, the universe dark flow.
Wherever it is taking us, let it blow.

Climate change

'Variable' is the approximate word
Used by new arrivals
Looking for the sun
After disappointing winters.

Old stagers take a wider view;
Grow to love this borderland,
Mix of hills and valleys.
Pressed, they might say it is benign.
Mixed weathers
Make for temperate climate,
Though capable of heat wave and of storm.

Recently, pure air from a distant region
Has encroached, signalling permanent alteration;
Requiring adjustment to daily living.

Old men are best placed for this transition.
Relinquishing the known, they become
Susceptible to the superior other; embrace
Meteorological indications
Of settled weather on the way.

Your silence

Your silence is a clasp of cloud,
A gathering of mist.
Insisted on, it grows its form;
Acquires mass, and almost could be weighed.
Would it have been so heavy if you'd stayed?

Mid-page, I set aside my book,
Switch off the light, sit back,
And step across the meeting line
Of your world's measuring and mine.

Mid-conversation, my ears rebel;
Head turns aside, as though I heard you call;
Or felt again the opening of your door.

Changing places

She was not Eurydice, after all;
And he no Orpheus,
Though he loved music and played a bit;
Not well.
And anyway, their roles had already been reversed:
He the stay-behind, she pioneering the upward journey.

Strange how sure he'd been
About turning the classic story
Upside down.

Nothing had been said about looking back,
Except that it would serve no purpose.
She'd left him in good order and he would follow.

And anyway…she smiled the thought…
Those flowers she'd left behind,
Geraniums, they'd conveyed her smuggled message;
Blooming extravagantly,
In spite of over-watering.

Gathering

It is calling, urging me,
That space, that somewhere,
Needing to be filled.
It is you-shaped.

These flowers, they feel it, too;
Blossoming outrageously,
As though they cannot do enough
To occupy the condition where you sat,
Still, silent, gathered.

It is about gathering, isn't it?
It's why you had to leave.
I could never get there
With your completeness so strongly occupying.

How much more grateful do we have to be,
Me and the geraniums,
Doing our best to fill your awesome not-here?

Edward Jones

Musical Offerings

Edward Jones

Songs without words

When words are gone,
There's still the song;
And the song is free to fly.

Words act as fence posts in a field;
Their grip is strong.

Now it's pure meaning, and the song
Is just the long
And lovely wordlessness we lie among.

*   *   *   *   *

Now that your words have gone,
Into the space they occupied
Comes something more than only silence;
Some truth, perhaps,
About the nature of our being.

In our long love,
Words swarmed like bees,
Like dark birds hovering;
Fragments of what we took for meaning.

Now there remains the long and lovely
Timelessness we lie among.

Our song

Life framed our love at one first sight;
Some simple scene, some movement caught
For all time by the transforming hand of Art.

We were recorded in a book
Where magic reigned.
And fairy tale, for telling and retelling,
Worked youth and age in timeless form.

Tale lived and loved,
Framed and bound;
Our song, our life, our love,
Among the scattered stars
Danced and sung.

On what enchanted wall
Does our framed image hang,
Awaiting consummation?

And in what silent reading room
Do we lie open, side by side,
Faithful to the waiting?

And on what final stage, I wonder,
Will we be danced?
Into whose arms, you ballerina,
Will you be leaping?

Music and silence

Your absence is the unworked score
On which I write the grace notes of my life;
And as in music,
Where silence is the unheard voice of time;
When played notes linger,
Those not yet born but somehow signified,
Are already being formed;
So your not being here imposes
Shape and line
On moments past and moments yet to come.

Silence and sound in concert sing
In equal partnership, their shared identity.
Absence and presence capture, as do words in rhyme,
Aspects of this condition we call time.

Music of the heart

When the music fades, and all
The business of performance drifts apart,
The essence of it stays with us to speak
Its own peculiarly holy word.
No need for programme notes or score;
The music sings its own perpetual encore.

You are the music of my heart,
Whose long rehearsal time has gone.
Variations on life's themes have dropped away.
I know you now as pure melodic line,
And do my best to sing in unison;
Accept your gathered harmonies as part
Of some perfected recapitulation.

Edward Jones

A musical offering

It starts with Bach, as it would have to do;
A scattering of notes flung by a royal hand
To test an ageing genius's invention.
And Bach's response to this unreasonable command
Was an offering not only to the king, his loyal band
Of cronies, but to the world, to me and you:
A gift beyond expected courtly due.

Now, Gubydulina fashions these same notes anew;
Each note its separate instrument announcing an intention
To create chaos, discord, violence and tension,
From which, in eight long minutes of heart-stopping beauty,
A violin would sing our spirits' magical ascension.

One final snarl of brass. The violin departs,
Fading at the peak of human yearning.
The maestro drops his arms, the baton rests;
And silence fills the hall, while in our hearts,
Echoes still linger, burning, burning.
And every still-remembered note attests
We have been changed, we have been added to.

'We are the music while the music lasts.' It's true.
But not enough. That music changes, too.
The music becomes us; it is me and you.
Natural as breathing, always on call,
It works upon each mind and shapes each heart;
As long as we live to nurture life and art.

If this is true of music, how much more love implies!
Lovers become each other, and their shared harmonies
Are their souls' music, which in love they prolong,
Fresh as the day Bach's genius wove them into song.

Edward Jones

Impromptu

Some days, when it's least expected,
Fingers for once supple,
Mind otherwise engaged, it shows itself, this thing;
What Schubert possibly intended.

Normally, me lacking application,
Joints stiff, touch gone, inadequate attention,
It never shows. Energy expended,
The thing lacks life, inspires no firm conviction.

'Keep practising, repeat the exercise.'
As if I were refining oil or forging dyes
From which a final product would appear,
Whole, miraculously clear;
What's left, just dross to be rejected.

But that's not how it is at all.
Missed harmonies and rhythms out of joint
Are crucial to that final score;
Universal counterpoint;
Mirror in which everything's reflected.
No more to be discarded than are stones
That form the path, or bones the frame.
That song will soar
Precisely as our tainted natures cannot be perfected.

Next morning, there they are,
Black notes, cold fingers,
Still on call.
Without their coarse infusions, nothing would sing at all.

Slow movement: andante con moto

Into the foothills of the heart we go,
With cautious steps the upward journey making,
As Brendel lays down chords, the silence breaking;
Delicate as feline sampling of first snow.

Outriders of the mystery we're here to share,
Invading places in our hearts we know
Exist, but did not recognise, or did not dare.

Key signature

Mornings, I wake to familiar routine:
Wash, dress and eat; go shopping;
Occasionally clean.
Afternoons, I walk or write,
Play the piano, occupy the day
Till supper calls, and reading.
And then the night.

Routines like this form lines and spaces,
Horizontals, verticals, tones and paces
Of my life's manuscript, for life to write
Stark black on white
And inescapable:
The frame on which reality might dwell
In terms of state of mind.
Might even tell
Particular awarenesses of you.

In earliest days of your being gone
These were the absolutes to which I clung,
Occasionally and perilously daring
To hang a note, a phrase, a tentative suggestion
Of what might grow into a song
Or satisfying chord: temporary, fleeting,
Never, it seemed, to be quite caught.

Now, I am in the company of Cage and Glass;
Of jazz improvisers, the minimalist brigade;
Where keys are lost, particular notations fade;
Lines and spaces blur, as do treble clef and bass,
As harmony asserts itself to occupy
All those surrendered places.

While musicology's prescriptive shapes
Excuse themselves and leave quite free
The spirit of the song to fly:
Bird pushing off from the supporting tree
To serenade the world's immeasurable sky.

Last song: No 3 Richard Strauss

Only an old man would deny us
This human too-much-asking.
We long for what is coming
But bear impatiently the waiting
For Strauss' genius resolution
Of long-enduring love and being loved and loving.

Only an old man would deny us repetition,
Knowing that repeating, being human, is retreating
From where this voice has brought us to;
Back to the world of time and time's diminishment.

This only-once is out of time,
Where only an aged man could let it rest.
And with it, only once, we sink, too;
Whether it is into sleep
Or into death.

Last song: No 4 Richard Strauss

Freed of all need for words,
This song,
Last stepping stone to silence,
Is purely telling,
One aged human to another,
About acceptance and ultimate fare-welling.

We who have lived and loved so long
Are out of words as we are out of time.
Only the vulnerable and tender
Female voice,
Generous as it is compelling,
Can render
This ageing heart's surrender
To our last need to be thus kissed away.

Partita

What certainties sustain these opening chords?
What truths behind this freedom from all words?

Be calm, be still, be reassured.
Give yourself to me, become me, relinquish thought.
Accept that I am Rightness, I am Pure.
Assimilate me, and be sure
That this confident beginning holds an accomplished end.

See me as product of the sculptor's art.
Hold me close that you may know
My texture, line and balance. So,

Feel me as Love, hold me as Friend.
Take the measured progress of my dance
As stately resolution of your heart's romance.

Let us proceed in harmony; follow my line of fire
Which rises, falls, turns turn and turn about,
Making its way beyond uncertainty and doubt.

Mine is a meandering line, or so it seems;
The kind appearing in habitual dreams
Of some perfection that your heart requires.
Know me, then, as Rule; accept me as Law;
But also as Unexpected, what Rule is fashioned for.
Follow me as you might a voice
Calling from some misty upland; and rejoice
That at my close your heart will hear
Time sweetly held in this, our Now and Here.

In France

To my children from Provence

Perhaps it was the Romans after all,
Not in the ruins at Orange or Arles,
But in the restless gusting wind
That etched my sight and thought with sand.

Or maybe those poor painters at their stalls,
Blind to Vincent's sun, who splashed and toiled
And missed the all-pervading wash of light
That blurred his lines of landscape and of mind.

Not really, though. They just prepared the soil
For that extraordinary place, the Clinique de St. Paul,
Where, facing Vincent's statue, and the sight
Of that existence-ravaged face, I felt it all:

This human fabric, daubed and tight,
Stretched in the glare of the Arlesian plane;
And in the cloisters remembered pain,
Which merged to light, and hung and pressed,
And made a reason for the wind.

All this was with me as I crossed the square
At Vaison, with your mother, at our rest;
And wanted everything for you:

   The restless gusting of the mind,
   The siren certainties of shape and form,
   The stained and painted anguish of it all,

If only, at the end, or somewhere on the way,
You could experience, as I had done that day,
A sense of light where human colour pales;
A whitening mode of being that prevails.

Le Murillon

Above the littoral, down weathered stone,
Varieties of greenery extend;
Mysterious climbers, brown and gold,
Embrace bright house-walls, door posts; blend
With early roses at the gable end.
Faded by south, irregular shutters fold
Back on the buildings' guarded bones,
Across dark rooms which shield the rising day
Against the restless brilliance of the bay.

Houses like these compel the serious eye;
Encourage valuation. in such affairs,
Not-knowing being the preferred state,
We feed on lost interiors, covert ways;
Areas suggested by what blurs the sight;
Permit ourselves to no more than half desire
For what our senses beg us leave untried.

We are not meant to live there.
Sunlight through those crooked grilles
Would blanch the faded roses of our walls.
Too sharp, too steep the arch and step
For this approximate flesh.

Visitors, our true location lies outside
Imaginary existences; we belong
In eyeshot of such images of time and space
As we long for and can cling to and can stand.

Toulon waterfront

Faced with all this,
What are we supposed to do?
Take note of everything on offer?
In some fashion make it ours?
For offered this world most certainly is:
It begs our attention,
And signifies a readiness to be inferred.

But surely there is more
Than mere interpreted possession
Asked of us recipients of the universe,
Artists of the given world?

For since this world exists and begs reprieve
From nature's natural law,
And we're key to its eternity,
On our stretched canvas its spirit is preserved.
Our noticing gives it form.

And we are canvas, let's be clear!
Not hand or mind that guides the brush.
Living canvas, surely, mysteriously aware,
But canvas all the same.
Our role is to be material,
Framed to receive, not interpose;
Treated to record, not for interpretation.

In France

For models, look in unexpected places:
Those imprisoned in a single cell;
The sterile, the weak: those for whom
Window-watching is the highest art.

For every second masterpiece demands
Courage which the mobile fit find hard to spare.
And light breaks through when faintest stroke
Works on its offered surface unimpaired.

Ales

The Cevennes surprised us, all right!
Not what the brochures conditioned us to.
Those polished crags all ready to bite;
Something hostile in the dark blue light.
And Ales, that was unexpected, too;
More lively, up-market, confident and bright.

But nothing was as new as you.

You took me equally unaware,
Drinking your espresso in that square,
Patch-worked with plane-tree light.
I had not looked to find you there,
nor catch all forty serious years with you
In one quick sight.
Though what could possibly be more true,
Since newness is your received condition,
And I have grown by such illumination.

It is not cities, regions, wives
Unaccountably get new.
It's our comfortably blinkered view,
Our tourist measure, our shuttered lives
Crack unexpectedly; let meaning through.

Under the vine

At Roque Gageac in Sunday sun,
Uneasily defined as English and as old,
We sat among French families, their weekly ceremonies,
At one with mingled heat and perfumed green,
And shapeless hum of voices, dappled light:
And sensed the indivisibility of things.

At Pont du Gard, age bleached in stone,
Mass lifted into weightless form,
Hung on the hot dry wind from Arles,
Wordless as touch, sightless as song,
We knew the insubstantiality of things,

Including and particularly Time,
The universe's pulse: now, then; here, gone;
Infinitesimal sounds of things
Inaudible to human ear, insensible to touch;
But flickered past the speed of light
To let its shadow fall on human mind.

Here, now, under this suburban vine,
Sun-scented and redolent of wine
From too-long-hanging grapes,
All Being shimmers into strengthening shape
Through us; one-souled and single-hearted;
Gatherers, folding into enduring form
The everlastingness of things.

With Reference to God

Duino

'It's hard being dead,' Rilke famously declared.
Spoke of its 'strangeness', too;
As though he'd been there; as though he knew.
Strange indeed! Yet I can imagine you
Sampling with joy that first strangeness
Which death had brought you to,
In that shadowed hinterland
Between my here and yours;
With yours smuggling a little of itself
Back to mine tracking your last steps here,
Your first footfall there,
Where the 'purely untellable things'
Might, perhaps, be told.

Oh, I have need to tell,
In this old Quaker house of prayer,
Where age-old lore
Concerning what should or should not be spoken,
May, at particular times,
Be broken.

A great stillness is upon me;
And a wide waiting, as though,
In my long-sitting silence, love,
Gentle for our intermediate condition,
Contrives for us to share
What we might take to be
First taste of immortality.

Quaker meeting 1

So here I am to give my thanks
Where thanks are due.
But thanks for what? For who?

For everything, of course, but most of all for you.

But who precisely do I send them to,
These thanks? How can I know
They're getting through?

We humans have this need to speak,
And though we're told, and surely know
Our lives speak for us, even so,
We have a need for words,
Something to show,
Get a hold of, aim where they're meant to go.
And even hope, such are our eccentricities,
For some acknowledgement that our vocabularies
Can manage to express our spirits' mysteries.

No chance! Better for me
To aim at being gratitude itself; a human strategy;
A wordless testimony.

Quaker meeting 2

That I should step aside,
Press against some convenient wall,
Not to impede the quietly proceeding spirit;

That silence should snow
On fields of words,
Eliminating features that disturb;

That movement in the mind,
Like an extensive traffic flow,
Should funnel to a halt;

That life should so impress itself
Through silent sitting, waiting without thought;

Amazes, comforts, satisfies.

Quaker meeting 3

Here we settle, centre down; allow
The small particularities of life to fade
Out to the margins.

As when some light prevailing mist
Permits the sun to filter through,
Warmth gathers almost surreptitiously. Our hearts
Expand, as though they did not quite believe
It could be so, this brief elusive presence of the real.

I never understood

I never understood what Rilke meant
About that solitary tree, the daily walk,
The habit that refused to go away.
How could they help when neither God nor man
Had anything to answer to my call?

But here in Shropshire, sitting still and small,
Day-by-day watching of one bone-bare, tall
And stricken trunk, stiff among tossing green,
Suggests a line towards the truth of things:
How they supremely and most simply are.

So how are they?
Ah, there's the rub. Sensing and telling
Require quite different tones,
And neither drops its secrets lightly in a word.

But maybe, by its posture...absence of intent,
Active affection or reflective grief,
Urge for progress, rise or fall...,
Sustained acquaintance with that lone tree's stance
Erases time; brings light from every quarter
Home to bear on now, here. This once-for-all.

Those who love

Those who love beyond their means
Are singularly blessed.
Faith is their immediate scene;
An everyday occurrence.

Being allowed a daily small advance
Of personal capacity,
Acknowledged retrospectively,
If ever,

Provides a practical model
Of our stance with God.

What You are

What You are cannot be known,
And matters not.
But that You are fashions the crown
Of every human hope.

Insist Your presence; be more weightily;
Prohibit deafness to prevailing tones;
Coarsen the language of silence.
Let it offend!

Precise direction, warning cones,
Degree of incline, final end;
All these the mind rejects when, gratefully,
Out of the foggy upland, heel
Strikes stone.

But if it's true

But if it's true that You cannot be known,
What are we doing, trying to comprehend?
Rats, it is observed, lose their senses,
Set in some impossible maze.

Humans, though, have a will to understand,
And searching forms dimensions of its own.
Not to engage becomes the sickness, in the end.

Even the blind eunuch's neutral gaze
Catches the scent of an imperial footfall;
The usher, showing us to our stall,
Clipping tickets, officially apart,
Surely is touched once the divine Mozart
Occupies the hall?

Getting to know You

Getting to know You is an oblique affair.
Those who would seek You must be sharp
On hunches and analogies.

Mid-conversation, a neglected face
Floats effortlessly to mind.
The habitual dog no longer barks.
Flowers modify their presence in a room.

Coming over the hill at nightfall,
There is the house. Smoke rises
From a chimney.

'Someone's home.'

Not knowing

Bees of the invisible, Rilke called us;
Ants of the unknown; workers in mystery;
Volunteers for service that's never explained.

Not knowing frees us,
Intention takes the place of grasp;
And mystery can work within us unimpaired.
Receptiveness becomes a kind of faith:
Not faith in something but the faith itself,
Which we are set to nourish
Within a scale of wisdom we can bear.

Even if one

And even if one of them, as Rilke said,
(Meaning an Angel), should clasp me to its heart,
I'd fade in the strength of its greater being.
And human minds work hard to hinder recognition.

These are not statements of regret;
Simply the way we are. Crumbs are our feasts,
And sampling is what we have to work upon.

These hints we get, being earthly stuff,
Confirm our standing in the scale of things.
They echo what we are; the bells they ring
Clamour among our almost secret places.

Have you not paused, on summer afternoons,
When music rises from suburban windows;
Or, unaware, sensed something absolutely whole
In human movement about a city square?

God's glance in our direction, these are scents
Of mystery we can feed on and to which we grow.

Other poems

Words to Rilke

This is the most terrible Angel.

One comes to terms with loss.
Sense of inadequate being gives a point:
The matter of gain or retrieval.
Not being loved is finite:
Exists or a gesture ends it.

These are the tangibles;
Experience confirms and diminishes them.
They are human.

But affront the darkest Angel, Love,
This heart-borne shape we cannot see,
Wholly! That is the terror!
One sees. One is allowed to know!
At the onset, one has arrived!

Each day's living consists in saying yes.
Our immortality, to have arrived;
And the obligation to go on arriving.
The discipline of heaven. Not rest.

Other Poems

Letters

Without these letters hammered to the page,
Pegs at appropriate angles,
This poem would drift away.

In rising fields, posts and rails,
Hedges and wickets mark intended quarters;
Snare seed, top soil, occasional harvest.

And then there's Rilke's tree;
A natural exclamation mark
Requiring a halt, summoning attention.

Not to those snagged deposits ripe for scrutiny,
Nor that interpreted song through branch and line,

But to stillness,
The wordless enduring being there.

Edward Jones

Autumn

Now it is Autumn and the trees are gold,
Our hearts are full of yearning.
How can we capture, how hold,
This incandescent burning?

Birds settle, day descends
In line with natural law:
A simple gravity which bends
All being to its core.

Not us! Our human greed transcends
This fall of earth and birds;
Need to interpret, grasp, amend;
Diminish being into words.

There is a noisy wind which blows
And strips the branches bare;
But that essential fire still glows;
Informs the autumn air.

If leaves were words and birds were song,
No trees would resonate
With inner light, nor heart prolong
What mind burns to relate.

Silence is the only tongue
With power to draw and bind,
In terms of timeless, voiceless song
Hungers of heart and mind.

Now it is Autumn and the trees enfold
This fruit of our discerning:
To stand and wonder, silently behold
The year's and our hearts' turning.

Dawn 1962

Why should this old reminder, dawn,
Speak so to my condition? Is it that light, like love,
Reveals, with lack of inhibition,
Day-truths that must be borne?

I can grow weary of this light,
Repeating what I can't avoid,
Each day, each endless day,
Facing the search and loss; destroyed,
The vision moving out of sight.

Failure and a certain falling short
Are part of small affairs.
Accepting this, we move in light;
Exist in our enchanting airs,
Little disturbed by thought.

But I am set another way to walk,
And have been so an age or two;
A way in which each dawn
Confronts me with the fact of you;
And truths I cannot baulk.

Nor want to; but the light
Comes sharp on trees worn thin.
No longer needing to be told
This love we're rooted in
Persists though we're in night.

Death will not bring an ease
Of such a search. No doubt
The thing goes on; the dark
And light turn, turn about.
Love ebbs and flows like seas.

Russian lessons 1958

Up Haverstock Hill I rode the tide
Washing homewards into Belsize Park,
Where frosted street lamps, smudged in dark,
Evoke some legendary pilgrims' way,
Past tall white houses multi-occupied,
Displaying plaques of names and bells
Suggestive of interior space, which tells,
Via basement flats and curtains drawn aside,
Of lives left casually on display:
An unmade bed, books here and there;
A woman combing long dark hair.

I steered around those siren calls,
On course for Emma's room:
Pre-revolution Petersburg princess,
Unlikely sorceress.
She held a winning magic hand
Of flaunting wild Cyrillic forms
That stalked across my grammar page
Like bird-prints set in tide-washed sand.

At that time, Pravda came from Moscow.
Nightly I picked at words, as if I were that bird,
Foraging for meaning.

While Hamlet's murdered father's ghost
Reared eighty feet above our city screens;
And 'Cranes were Flying' westward to the sun.

Other Poems

Daily to Finsbury Park I strained
To master those seductive runes;
Complex as crystal, hard as stone;
Fertile as fossils open to be mined;
Singly or in clusters, notes on a score;
Begging to be engaged with;
To be realised.

Marking time

This measured clock is marking time
In regulated beats upon a floor
Itself worn smooth by tread of feet
Marching to time's relentless beat:
The tap of drum, the beat of heart,
The pulse of tide along the shore.
The then, the now, the evermore.

Held out of time by beats of time,
Strings of particular silences contrive
A wordless, still and silent whole
Whose borderlands these marching steps patrol;
Where repetition's natural law...
The common round, the daily chore...
Erases time. We have been here before;

Where loss, long-mused upon, is gain;
And being-here grows out of gone-away.

As punctuated harmonies in music raise
The lifted, freed melodic line, each day,
Each regimented day transforms,
By repetition, into something more:
An elevated state of being, say;
Which grows, intensifies, is here to stay.

Index of poem titles

Ales	72
Authorpe 1952	20
Autumn	90
But if it's true	83
Changing places	50
Climate change	48
Dawn 1962	91
Departure 1968	30
Do not speak	40
Duino	76
Even if one	86
Freesias	32
Gathering	51
Getting to know You	84
Higher degree	42
Icarus	33
Impromptu	60
I never understood	80
In the shallows	44
Interlude 1	31
Interlude 2	37
I think of you	34

Key signature	62
Last song: No 3 Richard Strauss	64
Last Song: No 4 Richard Strauss	65
Letters	89
Le Murillon	69
Light out of dark	39
Marking time	94
Monument: Thetford Chase, 1960	26
Musical offering, A	58
Music and Silence	56
Music of the heart	57
Not knowing	85
Odysseus 1	12
Odysseus 2	13
On the beach	43
On Waxham beach	46
Our song	55
Palace Green, Durham, 1949	17
Partita	66
Penelope 1	14
Penelope 2	15
Prelude	11
Quaker meeting 1	77
Quaker meeting 2	78
Quaker meeting 3	79

Index

Return to the Old Rectory, Authorpe (1998-1952)	22
Russian lessons	92
Shincliffe Hall, Durham, 1949	18
Solitaries	41
Songs without words	54
Slow movement: *andante con moto*	61
Student Union, Durham, 1949	16
Summer gone	38
Those who love	81
To my children from Provence	68
Toulon waterfront	70
Under the vine	73
Watford, 1955	25
What You are	82
Words to Rilke	88
You 1968	27
You	28
You were not...	36
Your silence	49